STATIC ELECTRICITY
(WHERE DOES LIGHTNING COME FROM)

2nd Grade Science Workbook

Children's Electricity BOOKS Edition

SPEEDY
PUBLISHING

The study of lightning is known as fulminology.

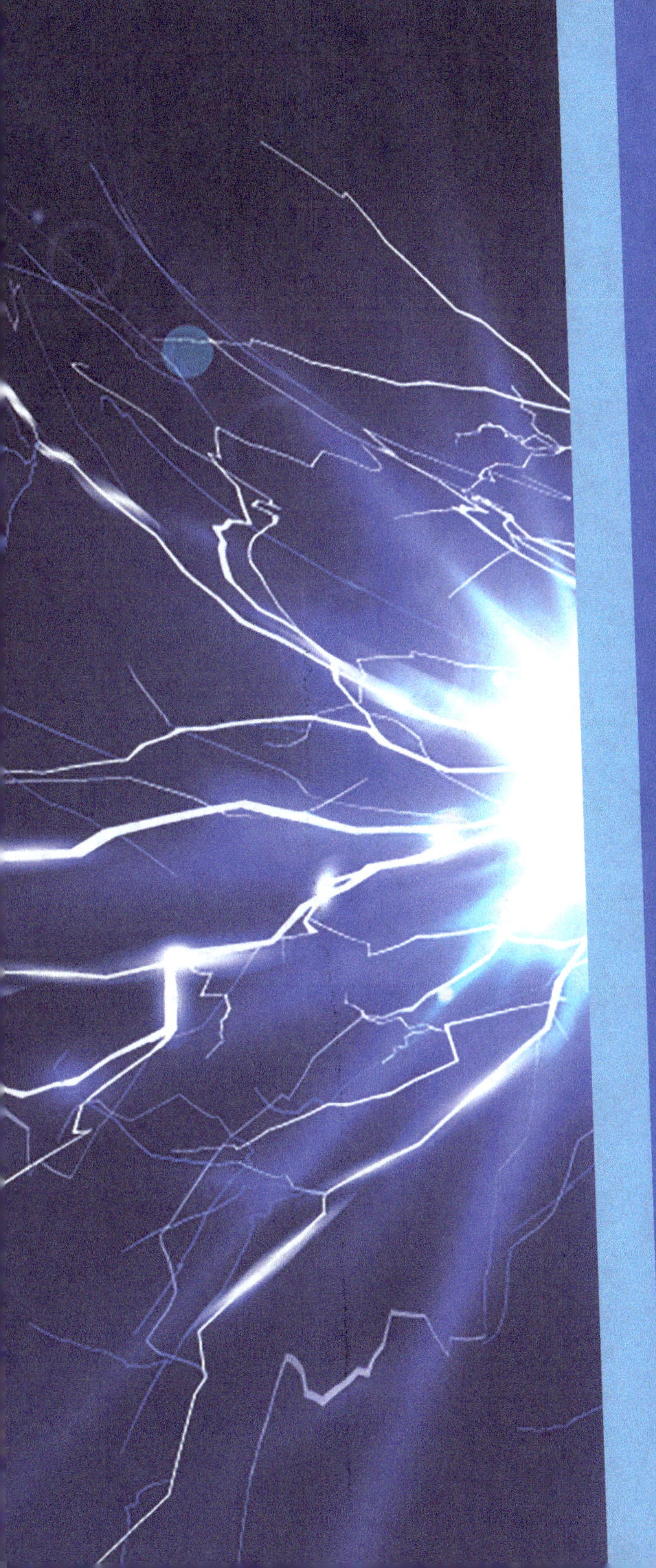

Static electricity is the build up of an electrical charge on the surface of an object.

It's called
"static"
because
the charges
remain in
one area.

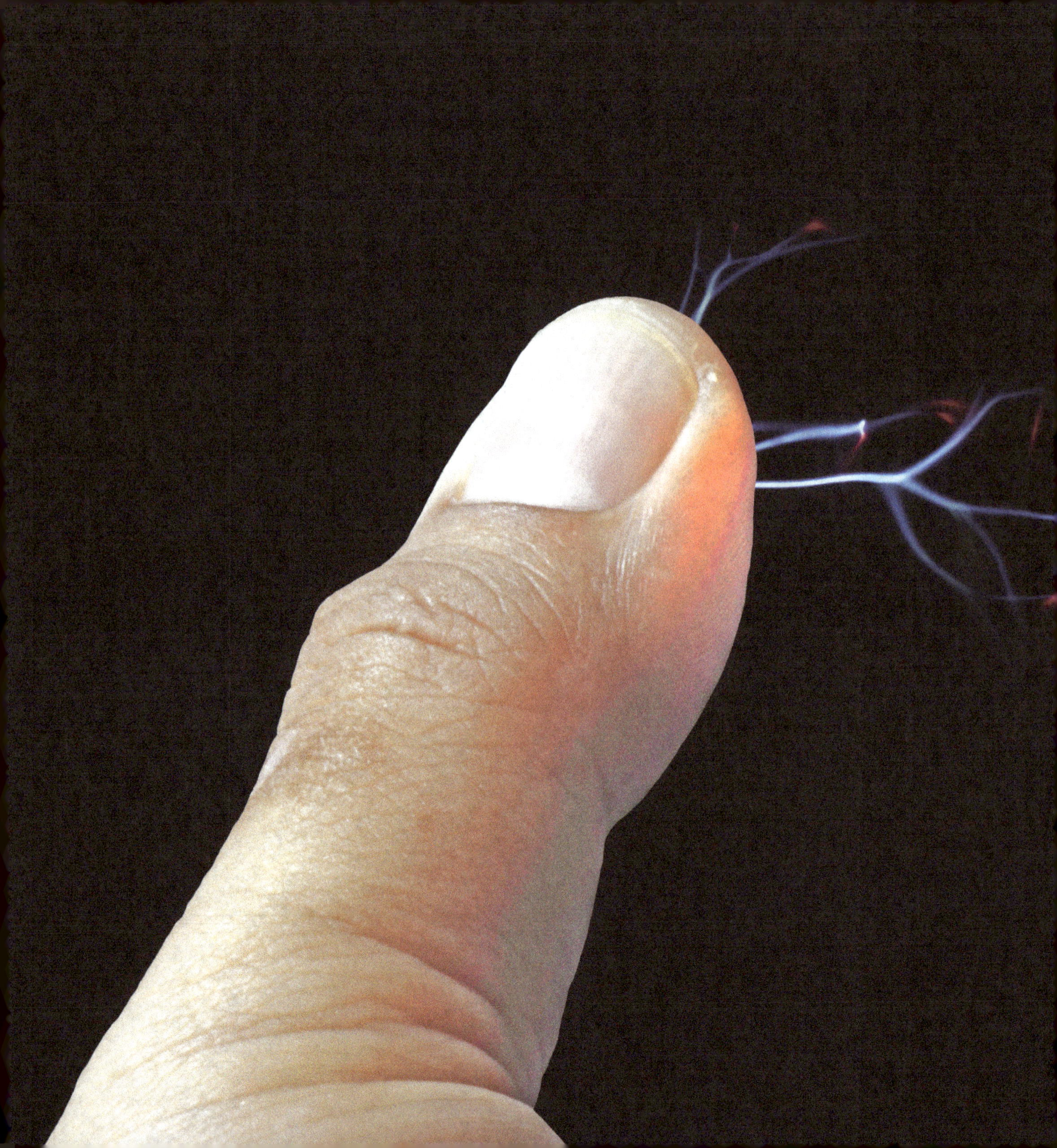

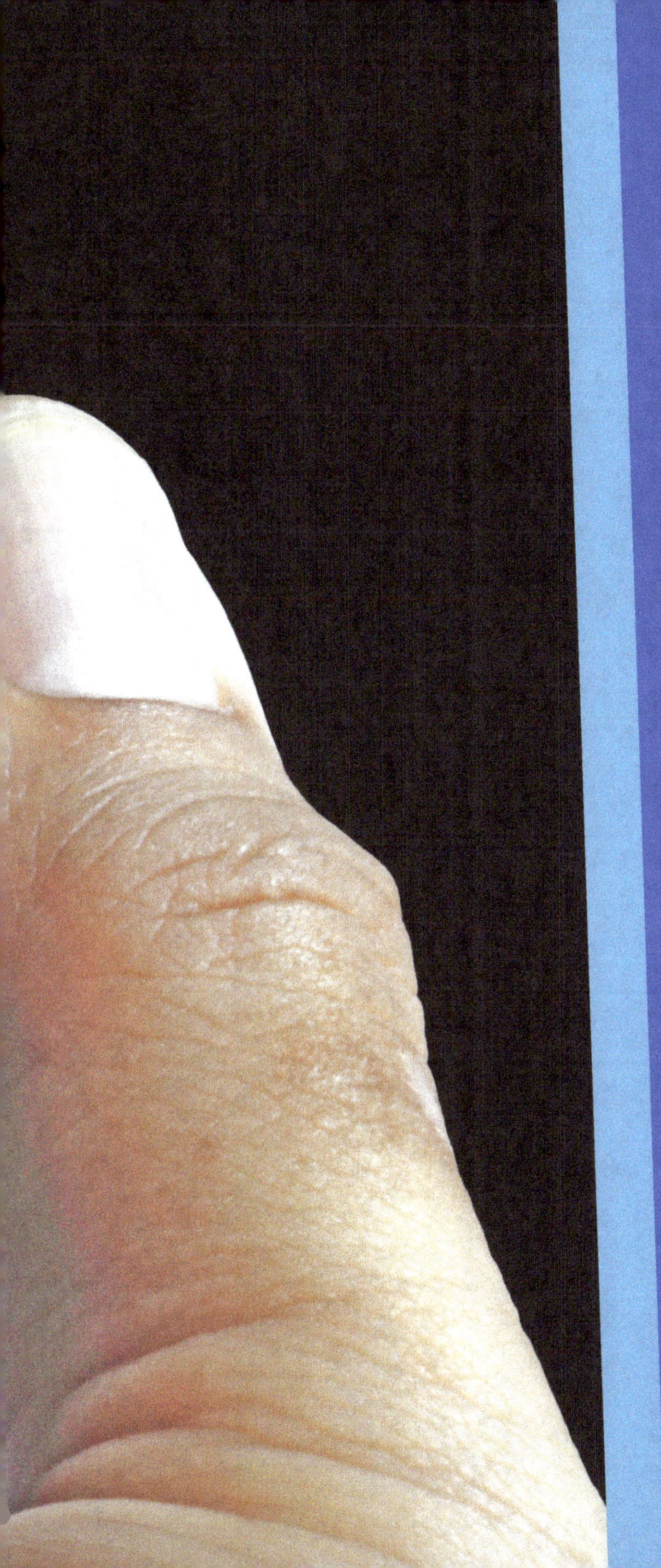

A static electric charge is created whenever two surfaces contact and the electrons move from one object to another.

A spark
of static
electricity
can measure
thousands
of volts.

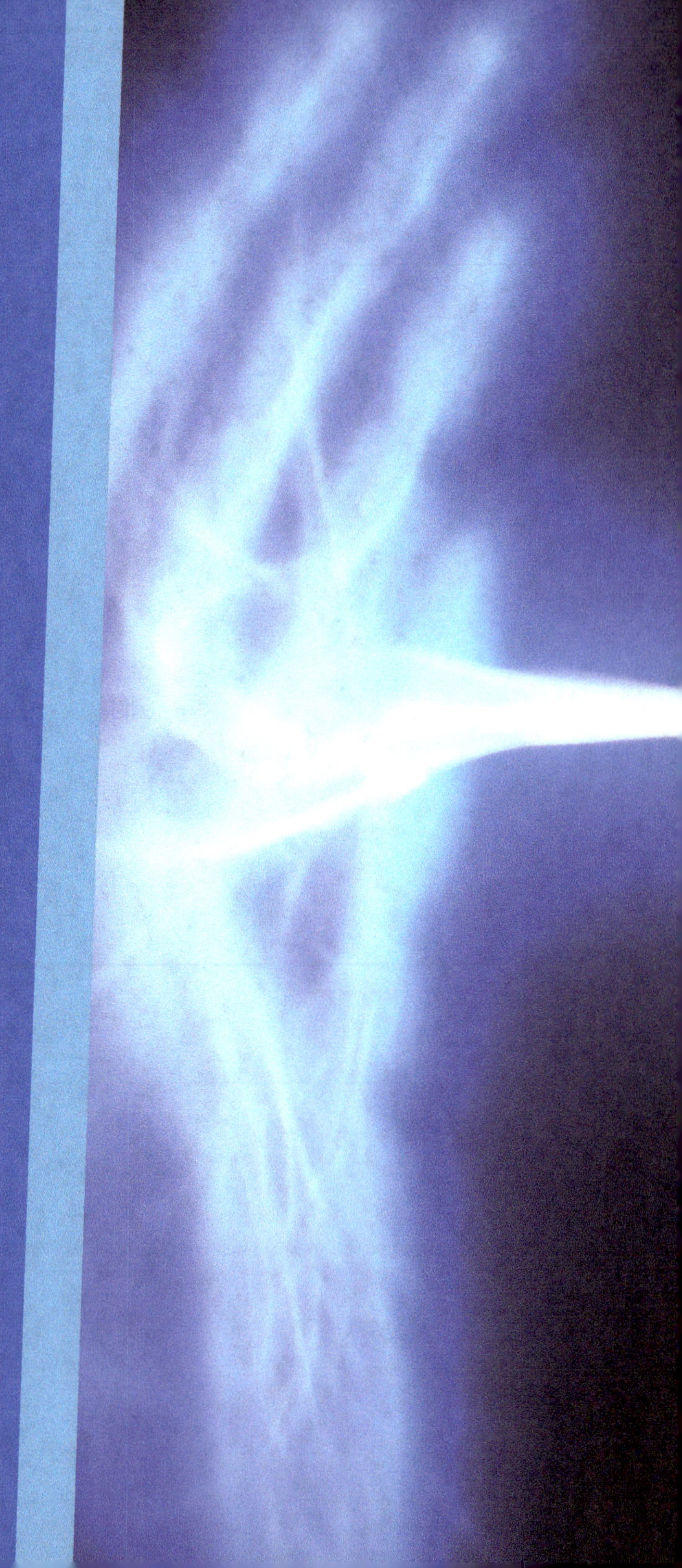

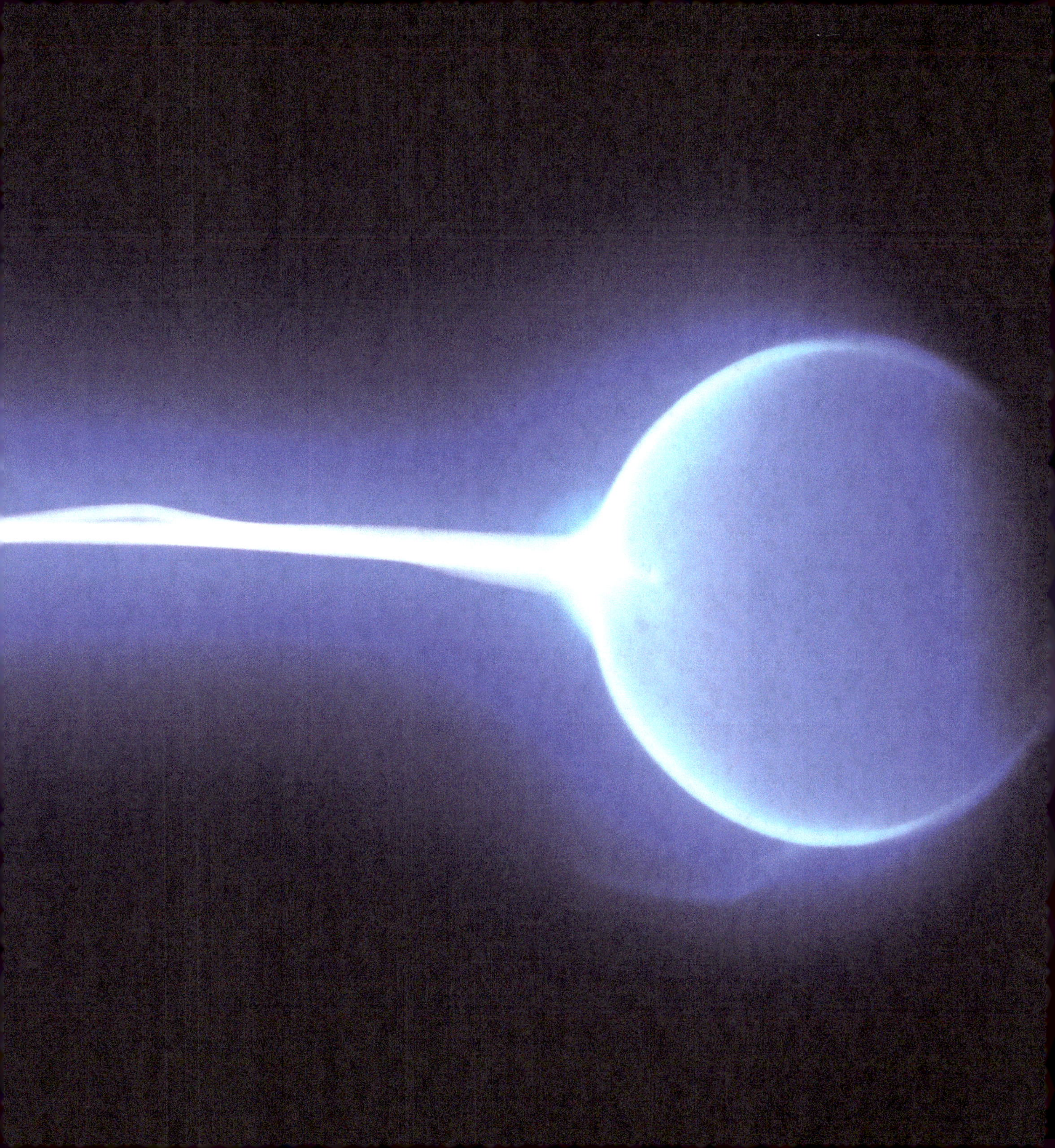

We see static electricity every day. It can even build up on us.

Lighting is also
a powerful
and dangerous
example
of static
electricity.

Lightning is a powerful burst of electricity that happens very quickly during a thunderstorm.

Lightning is caused by an electrical charge in the atmosphere that is unbalanced.

Within a thundercloud, many small bits of ice bump into each other as they move around in the air.

As they bump
into each other,
they create
an electric
charge.

When the charge connects with electrical charges on the ground, lightning strikes.

Lightning can occur inside the clouds, between the clouds and from clouds to the ground.

Lightning
is usually
produced by
cumulonimbus
clouds that
are very tall
and dense.

Lightning can
have 100 million
to 1 billion volts,
and contains
billions of
watts.

Most lightning occurs over land rather than oceans, with around 70% of it occurring in the Tropics.

The temperature of a lightning flash is 15,000 to 60,000 degrees Fahrenheit.

On Earth,
the lightning
frequency is
approximately
40-50 times
a second.

A lightning
flash is no
more than one
inch wide.

Visit
BABY PROFESSOR
EDUCATION KIDS
www.BabyProfessorBooks.com
to download Free Baby Professor eBooks
and view our catalog of new and exciting
Children's Books

www.ingramcontent.com/pod-product-compliance
Lightning Source LLC
Chambersburg PA
CBHW060145120726
48003CB00009B/3027